E A S T E R N
STEAM
IN RETROSPECT

V2 class no. 60912 of New England depot starts away from Peterborough North with an express train.
5.9.53

EASTERN
STEAM
IN RETROSPECT

ERIC SAWFORD

Sutton Publishing
First published in 2004 by
Sutton Publishing Limited . Phoenix Mill
Thrupp . Stroud . Gloucestershire . GL5 2BU

British Library Cataloguing in Publication Data
A catalogue record for this book is available from the British Library.

ISBN 0-7509-3499-9

Half-title page photograph: J15 no. 65474 approaches Huntingdon East station with a train of
wagons for various destinations on the East Coast main line.   16.3.54
Title page photograph: V2 2–6–2 no. 60826 blasts through Huntingdon on its
journey north.   8.8.54
Endpapers. Front: Peterborough North station bustling with activity.   8.8.54
Back: A4 no. 60030 *Golden Fleece* runs into Peterborough North station. This
locomotive was a favourite with Kings Cross enginemen, hence the polished buffers. 7.8.54

Typeset in 10/12pt Palatino.
Typesetting and origination by
Sutton Publishing Limited.
Printed and bound in England by
J.F. Haynes & Co. Ltd, Sparkford.

Contents

Standard 9F no. 92042 from New England depot in full cry on its journey north, having been given the main line at Huntingdon.   28.2.63

With the whistle warning of its approach, A4 class no. 60011 *Empire of India* heads the non-stop 'Elizabethan'. It had already slowed down to obey the 20mph restriction through Peterborough North station, and here youthful enthusiasts welcome this Haymarket engine. The service was operated by Kings Cross and Haymarket A4s.

5.9.53

The J15 class was well known for its haulage capabilities, and in their heyday these engines were principal goods locomotives for the Great Eastern Railway. Even in their final years many of these versatile engines were often to be seen on passenger duties. Here no. 65451 stands ready to depart from Cambridge with the Mildenhall service.

10.10.55

Introduction

From an early age I was fortunate enough to live in close proximity to the East Coast main line, and in the mid-1950s moved to a house where the line ran close to the back of the garden. One decision I made all those years ago was not to collect numbers but rather to record on film as many locomotive types as I could. I photographed engines from all the regions, but the Eastern Region always remained my favourite.

My early memories go back to LNER days, although I did not have a camera at that time. For me railway photography began in 1950 with a second-hand camera using 116-size film. In 1950 I purchased a new Agfa Isolette which produced excellent 2¼-inch square negatives. This and a later model were, for many years, to be my constant companions. Initially photography was confined to public areas. In due course I applied for, and was issued with, a lineside permit, samples of my work having been sent for inspection and an indemnity form signed. The permit was renewed annually and, over the years, the area it covered was considerably extended.

The permit opened up many more possibilities, and whenever I had time to spare and the weather conditions were good I would go to the lineside. You never knew what would turn up; nothing was more infuriating than to see something pass that you would dearly have liked to photograph. But it was much more satisfying than going round a depot, where particularly interesting locomotives were inevitably to be found in the darkest part of the building, or outside surrounded by wagons or in some other impossible-to-photograph position.

In this book I have set out to provide an overview of what the Eastern Region had to offer in the days of steam, ranging from the star performers, the Pacifics, to the small tank locomotives that went quietly about their business. Huntingdon of course features largely in the picture selection, not only the main line but also the cross-country route to St Ives and Cambridge. This was Eastern territory. The other way, from Huntingdon East to Kettering, came under the London Midland Region.

The main line was very much the domain of the Gresley and Peppercorn Pacifics, pride of place going to the King's Cross (Top shed) A4s. During the summer months Haymarket A4s would alternate with the London-based engines on the 'Capitals Limited' trains and later on the non-stop 'Elizabethans'. Only then did the Edinburgh engines appear on the southern section. One of these was no. 60009 *Union of South Africa*, which has survived to become one of the best known of all the preserved locomotives. The Newcastle-based A4s made rare appearances in London.

Many of the principal expresses were in the hands of the very capable A3s. Enthusiasts of the day were always on the lookout for those based in the North Eastern Region. A large number of these well-known locomotives were allocated north of the border. They were frequent visitors to Doncaster for general overhaul, even on running in turns prior to returning to their home depot. Only on extremely rare occasions did they come south of Peterborough. How many enthusiasts of the day I wonder would have liked to 'cross off' the four examples based at Carlisle Canal shed, *Sir Visto*, *Bayardo*, *Coronach* and *Flamingo*.

One class that was well known on the main line right through to the end of steam were the V2 2–6–2s. These powerful locomotives were called upon to handle numerous types of train, ranging from expresses through to heavy coal. If a Pacific failed either prior to leaving

the shed or en route, there was a fair chance that the replacement would be a V2. In addition, they were often seen on specials and relief trains. With 184 in service, spread between the Eastern, North Eastern and Scottish Regions, many enthusiasts tended to disregard them. How very different it is today when no. 60800 *Green Arrow* makes an appearance. I always photographed V2s if conditions were right. The same applied to WD 2–8–0s. I can still recall my friends' lack of interest and comments like 'it's only a Dub Dee' when a WD clanked by heading a heavy coal train destined for Ferme Park, or the return empties heading north. Some of the first Standard 9Fs were allocated to New England and soon found themselves on these duties, raising some concerns in the process. If the signals were against them at Huntingdon, they initially experienced braking problems running down the 1-in-200 gradient from Abbots Ripton. After a series of trials, modifications were carried out which solved the problems. In the late 1950s New England received a sizeable batch of twenty-five 9Fs. At this time there were still twenty WDs in service, sharing some of the heaviest workings with the Standards.

During the 1950s the majority of locomotives working south of Peterborough were Gresley designs, although locomotives of Great Northern origin were still occasionally seen. The very useful J6 class 0–6–0s were used on light goods and engineering trains. At quiet times and on Sunday mornings tank locomotives of classes J52 and N1 often travelled to and from Doncaster works under their own steam, as did the later Gresley N2 0–6–2Ts.

Standard locomotives other than 9Fs were rare until the early 1960s when Britannias, displaced from East Anglia, took over the King's Cross–Cleethorpes service. These were allocated to Immingham depot, replacing the immaculate B1s formerly used.

Kings Cross V2 no. 60828 resplendent in Brunswick green livery pulls smartly away from Huntingdon. This engine was later to move to the North Eastern Region, being allocated to York depot from where it was withdrawn in September 1965. After two months in store it was towed to Cashmores of Great Bridge for scrap.   12.6.57

Prior to its rebuilding, Peterborough North station had an overall roof and a curving platform, which required the use of a banker to get heavy northbound expresses away. For a number of years the elderly C12 class 4–4–2Ts introduced by H.A. Ivatt in 1898 were used for this purpose. I can well recall their sharp exhaust note, magnified by the canopy. The C12s were also responsible for working several branch lines in the area and for stock workings. Other locomotives used as bankers included a number of ex-Great Central N5 class 0–6–2Ts. It was always interesting to stand at the north end of the station and watch a heavy express get away. Usually some slipping would occur, especially if the rails were wet or greasy. The C12 or other banker assisted until the train was clear of the platform.

The Eastern Region did not grant permits to individuals to visit locomotive depots, so it was necessary to join an organised party. One shed that always attracted me was the largest in the region, Stratford. In the early 1950s it had an allocation of over four hundred engines. In addition there were always a number present awaiting or ex works, and usually some whose working days were over. They were destined for scrap. Prior to the arrival of the Britannia class the largest passenger engines at Stratford were Sandringhams. There were also sizeable studs of B1 and B12 4–6–0s but by far the most numerous were the N7 0–6–2Ts, principally used on suburban services. Ex-Great Eastern Railway 0–6–0Ts were also present in considerable numbers throughout the 1950s.

I became very familiar with the J15 0–6–0s, a class of Great Eastern Railway origin first introduced in 1883. These little engines were sturdy and powerful, and were to be found on many duties during the first years of the 1950s, including regular passenger work. One turn for a Cambridge locomotive was the first train of the day to Kettering and the last return service in the evening. The engine spent most of the day on Kettering shed or, occasionally,

The locomotives of the 04 class varied considerably but they were all rugged, powerful engines well liked by the enginemen. Many were built for the government for use in the First World War and were later taken into LNER stock. No. 63779, photographed at Mexborough, was one of these. Built by the North British Locomotive Company, it was completed in May 1918.   24.6.56

A small number of the J17 class engines were fitted with a vacuum ejector enabling them to work passenger trains. No. 65511, seen here at Stratford, was not among them. Built in 1900, it was superheated in 1923, and remained in service until November 1960.   7.5.55

Boston shed had an allocation of nearly forty locomotives for most of the 1950s. The majority were K2 2–6–0s and J6 class 0–6–0s. From left to right the engines seen here are 04 no. 63759 (with a K2 behind), WD no. 90495, J69/1 no. 68570 and (in the shed entrance) J6 no. 64244. Boston closed to steam in January 1964. 13.3.55

on shunting work. No. 65390 worked this service for several years and was fitted with an extra lamp bracket on the right-hand side of the buffer beam. Other members of the class were to be found on branch line duties in East Anglia. The Mildenhall service was another for which a J15 was provided by Cambridge. The depot had ten J15s in the mid-1950s, and all were kept busy. One was sent to the small sub-shed at Huntingdon East where two sets of enginemen were based. This engine was changed on a ten-day rota. Its duties were the Huntingdon pilot and local goods to and from St Ives. In the very early 1950s it also worked a two-coach passenger service in the mornings and evenings. At one time these engines were principal goods locomotives. On one occasion the Huntingdon pilot was called upon to take over a heavy London-bound express from an ailing A4. The J15 struggled south until relieved by a V2 commandeered from a goods train.

Another of the larger Eastern Region depots was Colwick, although it had only half the number of locomotives based at Stratford. This was principally a goods depot, with considerable numbers of 04 and WD 2–8–0s allocated to it. In addition there were several classes of 0–6–0 engines of Great Central and Great Northern origin. In the early 1950s these included most of the few remaining J5 class 0–6–0s. Colwick was also home to a number of B1 4–6–0s, K2 and K3 2–6–0s.

It was not long before I wanted to record on film other locomotive types that appeared in the famous Ian Allen ABCs, not just those to be found on the Eastern Region. So I began careful research as to the most likely places to see and, I hoped, photograph them. I was always interested in heavy freight locomotives, those true workhorses of the days of steam, as well as the few massive shunting engines originally built to work where hump shunting was in operation. By the early 1950s most were relegated to normal shunting and in some

Overleaf: The Peppercorn A1 class locomotives were powerful and reliable engines, well liked by their crews, but for some reason they never received the publicity of the Gresley designs on the main line. Here no. 60138 *Boswell* of York depot heads a northbound express at Huntingdon. 24.2.63

B1 no. 61179 with an evening fish train had already shut off steam on the long 1-in-200 descent to Huntingdon. One was left in little doubt as to the contents of the vans on such trains as they passed by.   8.9.59

cases were stored. This was the case with several of the S1 0–8–4Ts, four of which were in store at Doncaster in 1954 and I was lucky enough to capture them on film.

Every depot had in its allocation a number of small tank locomotives mostly used for shunting work, with others acting as station pilots or employed on stock working. They consisted principally of designs originating from the Great Northern, Great Eastern and Great Central railways. The Midland & Great Northern Joint Railway locomotives had been withdrawn by the early 1950s. At about the same time the Wisbech & Upwell Tramway in Cambridgeshire changed from steam to diesel power and as a result I found several of the 0–6–0T tram engines lying idle at March depot in 1952, together with a solitary class Y6 0–4–0T.

Tight curves required short wheelbase tank locomotives. In 1913 A.J. Hill introduced the sturdy Y4 class, especially designed for this work. Weighing just over 38 tons and with 3ft 10in driving wheels, they always gave the impression of having been built much later than they actually were.

Coal trains and other mineral traffic were commonplace during the 1950s, when collieries in many areas were still busy, and nearby depots required an allocation of heavy goods locomotives to handle the work. These big engines were also used to transport iron ore to steel works. The characteristic noise made by these long, heavy, loose-coupled trains as they 'buffered up' has long since been silenced. In those days many other goods were also carried on the railways, including livestock, fish and other perishables, pigeons and bricks.

The arrival of the 1960s brought many changes. There were numerous line closures, diesel locomotives became increasingly common, and within a relatively short time the steam depots were closed as steam was eliminated from the Eastern Region. When Doncaster shed closed in April 1966, the last in the Eastern Region, it marked the end of an era, although steam still worked in from other regions for a while. The pictures for this book have been carefully chosen to illustrate the various types of locomotive that could be found in the region during the 1950s and early 1960s, before steam vanished completely.

1. Passenger and Mixed Traffic Locomotives

S ir Nigel Gresley had moved from the Great Northern Railway to take up the position of Chief Mechanical Engineer of the LNER, a post he held until 1941. During his long career he was responsible for the introduction of numerous locomotive types. Those for which he is best remembered are Pacifics, especially the streamlined A4s and his famous 'maids of all work', the V2 class 2–6–2s. In 1941 Edward Thompson took over from Gresley. During his five years in office he rebuilt the A10 *Great Northern* and six Gresley P2 class 2–8–2s as Pacifics, together with a development of the latter as new construction. In 1942 he introduced the B1 class, a good mixed traffic 4–6–0, which eventually totalled 410 locomotives. It was to prove a popular and robust design. These and the 2–6–4 L1 class tank locomotives were to be major contributors to his standardisation plans.

Mr A.H. Peppercorn took over in 1946 and remained in office for three years, during which time the railways were nationalised. In 1959 the position was abolished. Mr Peppercorn will be remembered for the A1 class Pacifics, forty-nine of which were built in 1948/9 at Darlington works. These engines were a development of the A1/1 *Great Northern*, and five were fitted with roller bearings. The A1s were to become a familiar sight on the main line and were responsible for many of the principal expresses. They were well liked by enginemen, and although there were a few problems initially these were quickly resolved. However, they were never as smooth riding as the A4s with which they were compared.

A4 no. 60032 *Gannet* was running in British Railways blue livery when this picture was taken at New England depot. It changed to BR green in October 1952. The single chimney was replaced by a double in November 1958. *Gannet* was withdrawn in October 1963 and after a short period in store it was cut up at Doncaster in January 1964.   28.1.51

Heavy showers and threatening skies did little to help photography at Peterborough North as A4 no. 60030 *Golden Fleece* runs into the station. This locomotive was a favourite with Kings Cross enginemen, hence the polished buffers. In the bay on the left is a veteran J52 saddletank on pilot duty.   7.8.54

Opposite, top: A4 no. 60033 *Seagull* leaving Huntingdon with the 9.16am fast train to London. In the 1950s most of the London services called at stations en route. The 9.16am and the evening Cleethorpes service were the only two to run non-stop.   1.8.54

Opposite, bottom: The Kings Cross A4s were well maintained, as can be seen from this picture of no. 60034 *Lord Farringdon* leaving Huntingdon. Despite starting off from a standstill, the powerful A4s coped easily with the 1-in-200 gradient here. The engine would work back with an express. *Lord Farringdon* ended its working days in Scotland, allocated to Aberdeen Ferryhill shed.   21.6.57

Sunday mornings in the early 1950s would see a Kings Cross Pacific (or occasionally a V2) work the only northbound morning passenger train, returning south later with an express. This is no. 60017 *Silver Fox*, photographed at Huntingdon on this duty. Note the silver fox emblem on the side of the engine.   28.9.52

A4 no. 60008 *Dwight D. Eisenhower* heads down the 1-in-200 gradient towards Huntingdon on its way to London Kings Cross, as the low sun throws a strong shadow on the embankment. Although this was only a few years after the war, the track on the East Coast main line was already back in good condition.   4.10.52

A4 class no. 60014 *Silver Link* heads a Glasgow to London express through Huntingdon. On the right of the picture can be seen the end of one of the Huntingdon East platforms, a favourite spot for enthusiasts of the day. An L1 stands on the left, ready to leave with a pick-up goods for Hitchin.   5.5.55

A4 no. 60026 *Miles Beevor* speeds north through Abbots Ripton on a dismal autumn day. The two platforms here were staggered and were connected by an overbridge. As with so many other places nothing now remains to indicate that a station once flourished here.   3.10.53

The first northbound stopping train of the day on Sundays in the early 1950s was usually worked by a Kings Cross A4. This is no. 60032 *Gannet*, still fitted at this time with a single chimney.   21.11.54

Newcastle A3s occasionally worked through to London, as was the case with no. 60083 *Sir Hugo* of Heaton shed, photographed here on the 1-in-200 descent to Huntingdon. In the early 1950s the best chance of seeing a Newcastle engine was on the Glasgow express passing Huntingdon just after 2pm.   4.8.54

A3 class no. 60050 *Persimmon*, seen here at Sheffield Darnell shed, was one of three members of the class allocated to Neasden and used on the Great Central section. *Persimmon* was later to move to the East Coast main line and was withdrawn from New England in August 1962. 24.6.56

A3 no. 60110 *Robert the Devil* going in fine style shortly after passing through Huntingdon. This engine spent its final seven years allocated to Kings Cross shed from where it was withdrawn in June 1963. It was cut up at Doncaster works the following month. 21.6.57

A3 no. 60112 *St Simon* stands at a smoky New England depot, with the overhead water gantry connected ready to fill its tender. *St Simon* was a New England engine at this time, having moved from Grantham in 1962. It was withdrawn in December 1964, ending its days at Kings scrapyard, Norwich.   30.8.64

Opposite, top: A3 class no. 60046 *Diamond Jubilee* pulls away from Huntingdon. A New England engine at this time, the A3 was often to be seen on express duties. In August 1958 no. 60046 was among the first of the class to receive a double chimney, and German-style smoke deflectors were added in December 1961. Withdrawal from service was in June 1963.   7.5.59

Opposite, bottom: A3 no. 60105 *Victor Wild* pictured here in fine style at Offord on its way to London. This A3 was a Grantham engine – many express trains changed engines there at this time. No. 60105 remained at Grantham for several years until it was withdrawn in June 1963, ending its days at Doncaster works.   7.3.53

During the early 1950s the legendary A3 no. 60103 *Flying Scotsman* was allocated to Grantham depot. It is seen here heading an express bound for Kings Cross. In the foreground is the indicator board for the travelling post office dispatchers, so the pouches could be swung out. The receiving net can be seen in the distance.   4.8.54

The renowned Flying Scotsman, seen here at Cambridge forty years ago, when it was already in private ownership. Its presence created considerable interest as steam had already finished in most of East Anglia by this time.   1.10.64

New England shed was within a few months of closure when this picture was taken. The once very busy yards give some idea of the depot's importance; this was home to nearly 170 locomotives ten years earlier. Here A3 no. 60065 *Knight of Thistle* awaits its final journey. Its nameplates have already been removed but the smokebox door number is still in position.   30.8.64

Excursion trains were a regular feature during the 1950s, running either to the coast or, as in this case, to London. Many people took advantage of these trains which usually ran full. A1 no. 60157 *Great Eastern*, seen here at Huntingdon, had started its journey at Grantham.   1.8.54

A1/1 no. 60113 *Great Northern* leaving Huntingdon with a semi-fast to Peterborough. The engine was in BR blue livery but still had 'straight' nameplates; it received the crested type during the month that this picture was taken. In August 1952 it was ex-works, this time in Brunswick green. No. 60113 was a New England engine at this time.   5.5.51

Heaton depot A2/3 no. 60516 *Hycilla* stands at the platform end at Kings Cross ready to move off for servicing, having just arrived with an express from Newcastle. This engine was fitted with a rimmed chimney at this time.   13.5.51

A2 no. 60533 *Happy Knight* was completed at Doncaster in April 1948 and carried its BR number from new. It is seen here at Huntingdon with the rimmed double chimney that it received in December 1949. No. 60533 was a familiar locomotive, which for many years worked in and out of Kings Cross. It was withdrawn in June 1963.   6.5.51

The six examples of the A2/2 class were rebuilds of the Gresley P2 class 2–8–2s originally designed for working between Edinburgh and Aberdeen. They were found to be unsuitable there owing to the numerous curves and in 1943/4 Edward Thompson decided to rebuild them. During the late 1940s all were transferred to York and New England. Here no. 60506 *Wolf of Badenoch* pulls away from Huntingdon with a Sunday morning local passenger train.   8.3.53

Three of the A2/2 Pacifics were allocated to New England depot, including no. 60505 *Thane of Fife*, seen here heading a semi-fast London service just south of Abbots Ripton station. In its final years the engine received a lipped chimney. Withdrawal from service was in November 1959.   3.10.53

The introduction of the Britannia class Pacifics soon made a considerable difference to services in East Anglia. No. 70011 *Hotspur*, seen here at Stratford, was one of the batch allocated to Norwich. As with the former East Anglian engines, no. 70011 ended its days at Carlisle, being withdrawn in December 1967 after just sixteen years' service. 7.5.55

Opposite, top: The principal duties of the three New England A2/2 Pacifics were semi-fast passenger services. This is no. 60504 *Mons Meg*, photographed at its home depot. 13.3.55

Opposite, bottom: A2 class no. 60525 *A.H. Peppercorn* fresh from a general works overhaul at Doncaster shed. It was almost ready to return to its home shed, Aberdeen Ferryhill, where it remained until it was withdrawn at Doncaster works in May 1963. 7.11.54

The Britannia-class Pacifics were very rarely seen on the East Coast main line prior to the early 1960s, when a number were moved to Immingham depot. Their duties included the Cleethorpes–Kings Cross service, which they took over from B1s and which resulted in regular appearances of the class on the main line south of Peterborough. Here no. 70040 *Clive of India* pulls away from Huntingdon, its first stop on the return journey.   4.10.62

No. 70020 *Mercury*, another of the Britannia-class Pacifics, is seen here at Peterborough working a Home Counties Railway Society special to York. A Willesden engine, on this occasion it was standing in for the Princess Coronation locomotive originally requested. Steam had already finished at Kings Cross by this time.   4.10.64

The unique W1 4–6–4 no. 60700 had just been repainted in British Railways dark blue livery with broad black and narrow white lining when this picture was taken at New England. It only ran in this condition for a short time before being repainted green in May 1952. The tender was a streamlined non-corridor type that had previously been coupled to an A4. 28.1.51

I photographed the W1 no. 60700 on its return journey on several occasions but never managed to get a good shot of the engine working hard despite a heavy load. It remained unnamed even in its experimental days before rebuilding. 15.4.55

V2 class no. 60912 of New England depot had just taken over an express at Peterborough North and was starting away, assisted by the C12 class 4–4–2T banker working hard at the end of the train. In the early 1950s V2s were often seen on express duties.   5.9.53

Opposite, top: Doncaster V2 no. 60956 in grimy green livery pulls away from Huntingdon heading the 9.39am fast train to Kings Cross. This duty was normally worked by a Pacific. No. 60956 was completed at Darlington works in October 1942. It was later to move to New England, from where it was withdrawn in September 1962.   22.4.57

Opposite, bottom: Abbots Ripton was one of the wayside stations on the East Coast main line. Here V2 class no. 60906 had just been given the main line on its journey south with a fast goods. Next to the locomotive are two livestock wagons, once a familiar sight. Abbots Ripton closed in September 1958.   3.10.53

The enginemen on V2 class no. 60908 await the 'right away' from Huntingdon with a local service to Kings Cross. Gresley introduced the V2 class in 1939. Classified 6MT, they were equally at home on express work or goods. 24.4.55

Opposite, top: V2 class no. 60904 departs from Huntingdon North with the first Sunday train from Kings Cross. The locomotive had not yet received a front number plate. On the right of this picture is a container wagon of a type once familiar on our railways. This duty was a Kings Cross turn worked by Pacifics as well as V2s, and engines returned with an express. 28.9.52

Opposite, bottom: Only eight V2 class locomotives received double chimneys. No. 60862, seen here heading a fast goods south of Abbots Ripton, was fitted in October 1961. Time was running out for many members of the class. No. 60862 was withdrawn in June 1963, just a month after this picture was taken. 8.5.63

V2 class 2–6–2s were often to be seen at March working in via the Great Northern–Great Eastern joint line from Doncaster. No. 60925, a York engine, is seen here standing ready for its return journey.   13.3.55

Opposite, top: Ready for the road at Kings Cross shed, V2 no. 60921, a Doncaster engine, waits to work a fast goods north on a gloomy January day. Note the oil can that can be clearly seen. This engine was withdrawn in April 1963 and cut up two months later at Doncaster works.   3.1.54

Opposite, bottom: On a bright autumn Sunday morning V2 no. 60800 *Green Arrow* heads north with a local train from Kings Cross. This engine was allocated to 'top shed' for many years and was used on a wide range of duties, including principal expresses, fast goods and, on occasions, heavy coal trains.   4.10.52

Fresh from works overhaul, V2 class no. 60893, a New England engine, is seen here at Huntingdon heading a special transporting agricultural machinery. The train had stopped and was awaiting the signal to proceed on its journey to London.   7.3.53

Doncaster shed was one of the largest in the Eastern Region and was always a fascinating place to visit in the days of steam. In addition to the wide range of locomotive types in its allocation, you would also find there engines that had arrived for works attention or others outshopped and undergoing running-in trials. V2 no. 60976 was a York engine, locomotives from this depot being frequent visitors to Doncaster.   24.6.56

The V2 class was designed by Gresley and introduced in 1936. Although they were described as mixed traffic engines, they could handle heavy express trains and were frequently seen on these duties. No. 60830, seen here leaving Huntingdon with a local train to Peterborough, was one of the batch built at Darlington in 1938. It completed twenty-five years' service.   8.6.57

The V2 class 2–6–2s have often been referred to over the years as the engines that won the war. Indeed, they were often called upon to haul herculean loads around the country, a role that they took in their stride. Powerful and capable of a fair turn of speed, they were popular with enginemen. No. 60846, seen here at Doncaster, was to end its days working from St Margarets, Edinburgh.   23.9.56

Specials and relief trains were often worked by the well-liked V2 2–6–2s which were easily capable of handling heavy trains and which, when required, could produce a fair turn of speed. Here no. 60826 blasts through Huntingdon on its journey north.   8.8.54

Doncaster V2 no. 60889 heading a breakdown train at Huntingdon as the evening shadows lengthen. Note the veteran coach next to the engine.   4.5.51

On occasions any available locomotive could appear on the heavy coal trains destined for Ferme Park. Here B1 class no. 61200 is returning to its home depot, Kings Cross, and the fireman is taking the opportunity of a brief rest as it runs down the 1-in-200 gradient to Huntingdon. 3.10.53

Fresh from general overhaul is Kings Cross B1 no. 61200. I always welcomed the opportunity of photographing engines in ex-works condition as most never remained in this gleaming condition for very long. No. 61200 was among the large number built by the North British Locomotive Company in 1947. 23.9.56

Excursion trains to Skegness originating at Kings Cross were a regular summer feature throughout
the 1950s. In peak periods other starting points were also used. Here B1 no. 61113 stands at
Huntingdon with a special which originated there.   1.8.54

Opposite, top: Stratford shed, with over four hundred engines, was easily the largest in the Eastern
Region and engine movements were constantly taking place. B1 no. 61226 was a Parkeston
locomotive, one of nine allocated to the depot.   7.5.55

Opposite, bottom: Stopping trains were often referred to south of Peterborough as the 'parley'. Here B1
no. 61389 is seen leaving Huntingdon with the Sunday morning train to Kings Cross. The B1 was a
New England engine, one of several members of the class allocated to the depot.   28.9.52

During the early 1950s Hitchin L1 class 2–6–4Ts worked many of the Kings Cross to Peterborough local services but as time passed these duties were mainly taken over by B1 class 4–6–0s. No. 61393 is seen here leaving Huntingdon on its way to Kings Cross.   12.5.55

B1 no. 61003 *Gazelle* was allocated to Immingham depot. It was to spend some considerable time at March in company with an LMR class 5 4–6–0, presumably both having failed. March had already closed to steam when this picture was taken, although a considerable number of visitors arrived on most days, many from the London Midland Region.   30.8.64

Departmental locomotive no. 24 pictured at March. Formerly no. 61375, it still carried its smokebox number plate. Although these departmental stock engines were still capable of running light, their draw hooks were removed so they could only be used for their intended purpose, which was carriage heating. This B1 was condemned in April 1966.   30.8.64

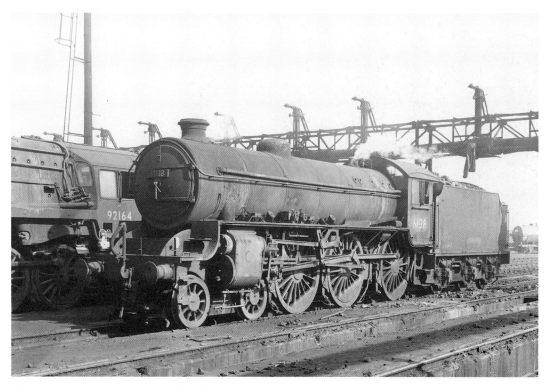

The overhead water gantry at New England depot must have considerably reduced the number of engine movements required as it carried water to all nine of the shed roads. B1 no. 61138 and 9F no. 92164 are seen here ready for their next duty. Time was running out as the shed was to close in just five months.   30.8.64

In the heyday of steam, Sundays would regularly see this end of New England depot packed with engines awaiting their next turn of duty, but by this time it was much quieter and only B1 no. 61109 and a 9F 2-10–0 were present when this picture was taken. New England closed in January 1965.   30.8.64

Several B1 class locomotives were transferred to departmental stock on withdrawal for use on carriage-heating duties. No. 61300 became no. 23, having been transferred to these duties in November 1963, and was condemned in November 1965.   30.8.64

Fish trains were a familiar sight on the East Coast main line in the early 1950s. They were frequently worked by K3 class 2–6–0s, later being taken over by B1 4–6–0s. Here, no. 61203, a Kings Cross engine, heads through Huntingdon bound for London.   1.8.54

Another special train, this time south of Huntingdon, worked by Hitchin B1 no. 61105. The B1s were mixed traffic engines capable of a good turn of speed, having the same sized driving wheels as the V2 2–6–2s.   1.8.54

Peterborough has changed considerably since this picture was taken in 1953. In those days the main line station was known as Peterborough North, and the other, Peterborough East, was still in operation. B12 class no. 61537 heads an M&GN line train. The tablet exchange apparatus can be seen on the tender.   5.9.53

Opposite, top: For several years two B12 4–6–0s were allocated to Yarmouth Beach shed, and both are visible here, with no. 61530 nearest the camera and no. 61520 behind. This picture was almost certainly taken on a Sunday morning, the most likely time to catch both on shed together.   18.8.59

Opposite, bottom: Ipswich shed had an allocation of eleven B12 class 4–6–0s, together with several Sandringhams. These were used on services to London, Cambridge and Norwich. No. 61577 is seen here at a smoky Stratford shed ready for its return working.   13.11.55

In the early 1950s the locomotive allocation of Yarmouth Beach shed was just eleven engines, including the two B12 class 4–6–0s seen here. Nos 61530 and 61520 both remained at the shed for many years. Note the tablet exchange apparatus fitted to the tender for working over the M&GN route.   12.8.51

Locomotives used on the M&GN section and other East Anglian lines required tablet exchange apparatus to be fitted, as can be seen here on D16 no. 62517 at Yarmouth Beach shed. Smoke must have presented a problem for the houses in the background if the wind was in the wrong direction   18.8.59

In October 1949 'Royal Claud' locomotive no. 62618 was repainted in LNER green livery with the lion and wheel emblem, joining the other 'Royal' engine (no. 62614). D16 no. 62618 only ran in this condition for a short time before receiving BR black lined-out livery as applied to its classmates. The engine is seen here at St Ives heading a Cambridge train.   17.4.51

Enthusiasts on Cambridge station in the early 1950s did not have to wait long for a 'Claud' to pass through, as Cambridge shed had sixteen of these D16 4–4–0s in its allocation. 'Clauds' were responsible for many of the passenger services in East Anglia. No. 62566 is seen here at the head of a Kings Lynn train. Note the white headcode disc and the clerestory roof on the first coach.   24.7.51

An immaculate K1 class 2–6–0 no. 62020 from March depot heads for home through St Ives with a mixed goods train. In the background is Meadow Lane crossing which was always busy with sand and gravel lorries.   17.3.54

Opposite, top: This is K1 no. 62038 awaiting its next turn of duty at March shed. This engine was one of several fitted with electric lighting powered by a Stone's steam generator; this can be seen alongside the smokebox just in front of the steam pipe. The equipment was later removed from a number of the K1s.   13.3.55

Opposite, bottom: Twenty-five K1 class 2–6–0s were allocated to March shed in the mid-1950s. Their varied duties included goods traffic to Temple Mills. Although they were mixed traffic engines, they were not often seen on passenger duties. All the members of the seventy-strong class were built by the North British Locomotive Company. No. 62018, seen here at March, was completed in July 1949 and withdrawn in March 1964.   13.3.55

One of March depot's K1 class 2–6–0s, no. 62051, drifts past St Ives with a train of empty coal wagons. In addition to its allocation of twenty-five K1s, March also had a sizeable number of WD 2–8–0s and ex-Great Eastern Railway 0–6–0s.   8.11.52

All of March depot's K1 class 2–6–0s had long since gone when this picture was taken as the depot was officially closed to steam by this time, but visitors still worked in. No. 62060 was one of two York engines present at March on this day.   30.8.64

Boston shed often used its K2 2–6–0s on passenger services, and here no. 61731 approaches Peterborough North. The LNER stencilled each locomotive's home depot on the buffer beam, a practice that continued at some sheds well into BR days although by this time engines were also carrying a shed plate, in this case 40F.   7.8.54

Colwick shed had nineteen K2 class 2–6–0s in its allocation, no. 61754 being one of them. Introduced in 1914, K2s were also to be found in the Scottish Region. Those north of the border mostly had side-window cabs.   4.4.54

Bright as a new pin, K3 2–6–0 no. 61838 of Immingham depot had just received a general overhaul at Doncaster works. The K3s were powerful mixed traffic locomotives, classified 6MT, with a tractive effort greater than that of the B1s and the class 5 LMR 4–6–0s which were both 5MTs.   24.6.56

In the early 1950s the large-boilered K3 class 2–6–0s were often to be seen heading fast goods. Sadly they were soon replaced by B1 4–6–0s and were then only rarely seen on the southern section of the East Coast main line. Here no. 61890 heads for London on a Sunday morning.   8.3.53

K3 class no. 61975 heads through Nottingham Victoria with a coal train. This locomotive was one of seven K3s allocated to Annesley depot and it was still there at the end of the 1950s. These were very useful engines and were to be found at many Eastern Region sheds.   6.11.50

K3 class no. 61943 heads a mixed goods for Temple Mills round the curve at Meadow Lane, St Ives. Goods traffic to and from London was routed round the St Ives loop to avoid congestion on the Ely line.
                                      17.3.54

The mixed traffic K3s had a reputation for rough riding, especially when they were due for works. No. 61978, seen here at March, was one of the last batch built. It was completed at Darlington in November 1936. 13.3.55

The March K3s were responsible for many of the freight trains to Temple Mills. The depot had a sizeable number of both the K3 2–6–0s and the later K1s. No. 61850 was built at Darlington in 1935 and remained in service until June 1963. 13.3.55

Peterborough North station is bustling with activity as Ivatt 4MT no. 43088 arrives with a train of vintage stock on an M&GN service, a J52 waits to attach a parcel van to a northbound express, and further on a Pacific stands ready for an engine change.   8.8.54

Opposite, top: The Ivatt 4MT 2–6–0s were the principal motive power on the M&GN section right up to the end of steam. They were fitted with tablet exchange apparatus, as seen in this picture of no. 43063 at New England depot.   13.3.55

Opposite, bottom: Fresh from its first general overhaul, Ivatt 4MT 2–6–0 no. 43150 stands proudly at Doncaster shed. Built in 1951, it was a Melton Constable engine at the time. The tablet exchange apparatus for use on the M&GN line can be seen on the front of the tender.   7.11.54

The Standard 4MT 2–6–0s of the 76XXX series were a development of the Ivatt design. No. 76046 was built at Doncaster and is seen here at New England during running-in prior to going to its first depot north of the border.   13.3.55

Several E4s were fitted with improved cabs (including a side window) when they transferred to the North Eastern area. Among their duties was the difficult Darlington to Penrith and Tebay route. No. 62781 ended its working life at Cambridge, spending a period of time in store before being withdrawn in January 1956.   19.3.55

Two E4 class 2–4–0s and two F6 class 2–4–2Ts were to be seen in store at Cambridge for a considerable period. E4 no. 62786 was built at Stratford in 1895 and completed over sixty years' service; it was withdrawn in July 1956. Widely known as 'Intermediates', E4s were allocated to many depots in GER days.   19.3.55

Only eighteen of the hundred-strong class of E4 2–4–0s passed into British Railways ownership. No. 62780 was the oldest of these, having been completed at Stratford works in April 1891. This engine was fitted with a vacuum ejector from new. The unsightly stovepipe chimney fitted during the early 1940s was retained until the engine was withdrawn in September 1955.   28.6.55

In the early 1950s the usual motive power for the Mildenhall branch consisted of the E4 2–4–0 class and J15 0–6–0s. When this picture was taken at Cambridge E4 no. 62785 was in charge, and it is seen here waiting to depart with the afternoon train.   5.5.51

York shed had a sizeable number of the B16 class 4–6–0s in its allocation. They were frequent visitors to the Eastern Region, not just to Doncaster where this picture was taken, and were also to be seen on the Great Central lines and occasionally in London. No. 61472 was a B16/3: these were rebuilds with three Walschaerts gears, introduced in 1944.   24.6.56

2. The Heavy Gang – Freight Locomotives

Heavy freight trains were a common sight in the 1950s and 1960s. Many were made up of loose-coupled stock, hence the sounds of 'buffering up' as they trundled along on their often slow journeys. These trains could be held in sidings if they lost their path or traffic generally was heavy, especially in areas such as the Fens south of Peterborough where they had to use the main line.

British Railways had the foresight to purchase a considerable number of ex-Ministry of Supply 'Austerity' 2–8–0s, widely known as WDs. These strengthened considerably the 2–8–0s of various types already in service. The WDs became well known for their characteristic 'clanking'. On the southern section of the East Coast main line they were the principal heavy goods engines until the arrival of the Standard class 9F 2–10–0s. In other parts of the region 0–6–0s were still employed on heavy freight trains. March depot used its J20 class engines to Temple Mills, working in conjunction with WD 2–8–0s and K3 class 2–6–0s. Pick-up goods and secondary lines were often the domain of the 0–6–0s of the three companies that amalgamated into the LNER in 1923, the Great Northern, Great Central and Great Eastern.

One heavy goods type that deserves to be regarded as a classic locomotive design is the 04 class introduced by J.G. Robinson to the Great Central Railway in 1911; many were not withdrawn until well into the 1960s. The Railway Operating Division in the First World War chose this design and had a large quantity built. A considerable number of these were taken into LNER stock from 1924, while others were to find themselves working in distant parts of the world.

Large numbers of goods locomotives were required at this time to handle coal and other mineral traffic, as well as the many other types of load dispatched by rail at that time.

In June 1951 J3 class no. 64116 ran into trouble at Huntingdon. The locomotive and all but one set of the tender wheels were off the track. No. 64116 was built by Dubs & Company for the Great Northern Railway and was completed in February 1898. In their heyday the J3s were known as 'Standard goods' and they were used for heavy goods trains, often double-heading. By the 1950s they were usually to be found on local goods, trip workings and engineers' trains. No. 64116 was withdrawn in 1952.   10.6.51

The J6 class was to be seen on numerous duties. First introduced in 1911, with 110 being built, they were allocated to many depots. No. 64254 was a New England engine, and like others at that depot it was fitted with tablet exchange apparatus to work on the M&GN section.   13.8.55

J5 class locomotives were fitted with the distinctive Great Northern-style chimneys. No. 65494, seen here at Colwick, was the last but one to be withdrawn. The J5s were also used on passenger work, especially excursion traffic to the Lincolnshire coast.   4.4.54

Another casualty awaiting attention at Doncaster. J6 class no. 64179 had run hot and had been towed out into the yard to await its turn in the workshops. Over the years I encountered several J6s with this problem – evidently it was not uncommon. 23.9.56

J6 no. 64180, a Boston engine, had just received attention at Doncaster and was ready to return to its home depot. No. 64180 was one of the initial batch built, being completed at Doncaster in November 1911. It remained in service until March 1960. 23.9.56

The Great Northern Railway introduced several 0–6–0 designs, but none was more successful than the J6 class. These engines made their appearance in 1911 and all survived to be taken into British Railways stock. Withdrawals commenced in August 1955 but it was 1962 before the class became extinct. No. 64197 was one of seven allocated to Hitchin, where this picture was taken.   14.10.56

Opposite, top: Every time I visited Doncaster I found at least one J6 0–6–0 in this condition. Here, one set of driving wheels had been removed from no. 64252 for attention, together with some of the coupling rods.   24.6.56

Opposite, bottom: The J6 working the afternoon pick-up goods was only to be seen at Huntingdon East station on the very rare occasions when it needed to take water. Here, no. 64186 waits to proceed on its journey south. At this time Huntingdon East still consisted of three platforms, but only the 'Midland' platform on the right of the picture was in regular use by passenger trains. Despite this, all three were adorned with excursion posters.   12.5.55

Eight J4 class 0–6–0s were taken into British Railways stock, two of which only survived long enough to receive their BR number. No. 64112 was one of them. This engine was built at Doncaster works in 1896. Unfortunately, I had only one opportunity to photograph this veteran at work, and then it was just two months from withdrawal. Most of its final service was on engineers' trains, as here at Huntingdon. Much to my surprise it had been given the main line for the long climb to Abbots Ripton. 6.10.51

The J1 class was introduced by H.A. Ivatt in 1908, principally to work fast goods trains. Fifteen were built at Doncaster, all in 1908, and withdrawals commenced before nationalisation in 1947. No. 65013, seen here at Hitchin, was the last survivor and spent most of its final years on engineers' trains. On several occasions, however, it also worked passenger trains and even took over an express from a failed locomotive. This gallant engine was withdrawn in November 1954.   3.1.54

Most of the engines on Doncaster's scrap road were tank locomotives. One exception was J5 no. 65480, which was withdrawn in October 1954 from Colwick shed. The smokebox door handle was missing but otherwise the engine was still intact.   7.11.54

The J5 class comprised just twenty locomotives built at Doncaster in 1910, but all survived to be taken into British Railways stock. In their heyday they were often used on heavy freight trains, notably hauling coal trains from the Nottinghamshire collieries to London. No. 65494 is seen here at Colwick. Withdrawals commenced in 1953, and the last example went in 1955.   4.4.54

This is J6 class no. 64186 ready to leave on its return journey to Hitchin, picking up at several points en route. To regain the Up slow line it had to cross over the busy East Coast main line. J6s were the last of the ex-Great Northern Railway 0–6–0s in service.   2.5.55

Opposite, top: During the 1950s March shed had just two J15 class 0–6–0s in its allocation. No. 65356 was built in 1888 at Stratford works and completed a remarkable sixty-nine years in service. J15s were to be found in larger numbers at Cambridge, which was the second largest shed in the March motive power district.   13.3.55

Opposite, bottom: J15 class no. 65438 is seen here on carriage pilot duties at Cambridge station. Completed in September 1899, it had been fitted with a side-window cab and a back cab on the tender. It was also fitted with a vacuum ejector which enabled it to work passenger trains. No. 65438 was a Cambridge engine at this time. It was withdrawn from service in June 1958.   21.7.51

The J15s were sturdy and powerful 0–6–0s, well liked by enginemen, with numerous herculean haulage feats to their credit. They were still widely used in East Anglia during the mid-1950s on passenger duties. No. 65473, seen here at Bury St Edmunds, was one of the youngest members of the class. Completed at Stratford in June 1913, it remained in service until March 1960.   21.7.55

One of Cambridge depot's J15s was out-stationed for a ten-day period working the Huntingdon pilot duty which in the early 1950s still included a two-coach passenger service between Huntingdon East and St Ives. No. 65451 was one that was often seen on this turn. The J15 used the small single road shed at Huntingdon East and was in the hands of two crews who lived locally.   15.6.55

Huntingdon station prior to rebuilding. The 'pilot' J15 no. 65457 stands alongside a loading dock. The island platform, footbridge, water tank and Huntingdon East (in the distance) have all gone and the present Down platform is roughly where the J15 is standing. 22.1.53

No. 65479 was the only J15 class 0–6–0 allocated to Hitchin depot. It was the last example of the class to be built, being completed at Stratford in September 1913. Together with E4 2–4–0 no. 62785, it worked RAF leave trains on the Henlow branch, and on occasions worked engineers' trains to Connington tip. No. 65479 was withdrawn in August 1960. 3.1.54

J15 class no. 65390 completed a remarkable sixty-eight years' service. Built at Stratford works in October 1890, it was among those fitted with a vacuum ejector and used on passenger trains. It is seen here taking water at Huntingdon East station.   15.9.51

The J15s were principal goods locomotives in their day. Many were fitted with steam brake only, while others, including no. 65449 seen here at Stratford, were equipped to work passenger trains. During the early 1950s they could often be seen on this work in various parts of East Anglia.   7.5.55

A small sub-shed was located near Huntingdon East station for the local pilot engine. No. 65451 was a regular on this duty. Built in 1906, it completed fifty-three years' service and was among those with Westinghouse brake and vacuum ejector fitted. 15.4.55

During the early 1950s the afternoon goods train from St Ives consisted of wagons that would be forwarded to destinations both north and south on the East Coast main line. Here J15 no. 65474 approaches Huntingdon East station. The entire train would have to be shunted across the main lines to reach the goods yard. 16.3.54

Locomotives from Colchester depot were not a regular sight at St Ives. J19 class no. 64650 was working hard as it hauled a train of empties round the curve near Meadow Lane. The J19s were introduced in 1912 and subsequently rebuilt with round-topped boilers.   17.3.54

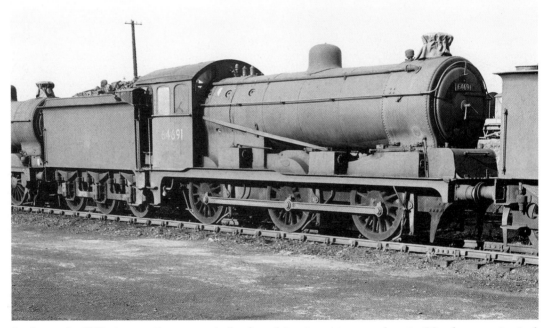

In the early 1960s locomotives were to be found in store at many depots. March was a typical example. No. 64691 was one of several members of the J20 class there, most of which never worked again. As can be seen, the locomotive was coaled up and its chimney protected, so it could have been returned to service at short notice.   9.9.62

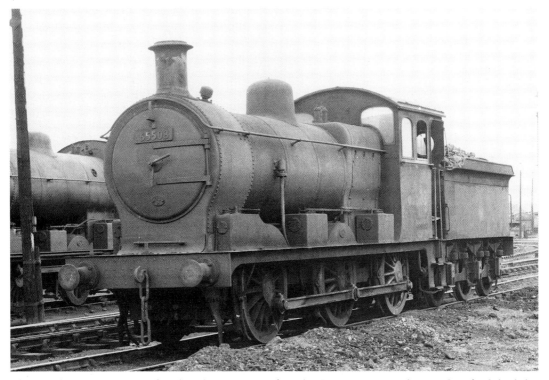

The J17 class engines were fitted with two types of tender. No. 65508, seen here at Stratford, had the 2640-gallon type, which had been fitted with a tender weatherboard. Originally built at Stratford as a J16 class in 1900, it was rebuilt to J17 and fitted with a superheater in 1929. Withdrawals of the J17s commenced in 1954, with no. 65508 remaining in service until June 1958. 7.5.55

Locomotives fresh from Stratford works were to be found on the running shed before returning to their home depot. J17 no. 65571 and D16 no. 62544 would not have remained in this immaculate condition for long. J15 no. 65473 had arrived for works attention, and it was to remain in service for a further five years. 7.5.55

Over the years I have seen many different types of locomotive on pilot duties at Cambridge, ranging from small tank engines to much larger types that were normally found on freight working, such as the J19 class no. 64654 seen here. The J19s were rebuilds of a design introduced in 1912.   21.7.51

Eighty-nine J17 class locomotives passed into British Railways stock. They were originally built for handling loose-coupled freight trains, but seventeen of them, including no. 65533, were later fitted to work passenger trains. This engine was one of five equipped with Hudd ATC gear enabling them to work on the LTS section. The vacuum reservoir can be seen in front of the cab.   7.5.55

Five J17 class 0–6–0s were fitted with tender cabs, and these locomotives were used on the two branches where no turntables were available. No. 65575 of Cambridge shed is seen here on shunting duties at St Ives, and its tender cab can be clearly seen. This engine was completed at Stratford in February 1906 and withdrawn in February 1958.   17.7.54

J11 no. 64365 fresh from its last general overhaul. Despite its immaculate condition, it only had a further three years left in service. Designed for use with goods trains, the J11 class engines were often seen on passenger services and they proved popular with the enginemen. During the First World War a number were sent to France, all of which returned safely.   24.6.56

The J11 was designed for the Great Central by J.G. Robinson and introduced in 1901. All the locomotives in the class were built either in the Great Central's own Gorton works or by four private companies. No. 64425, seen here at Barnsley, was constructed at Gorton in 1907. The class as a whole enjoyed a long history and examples were allocated to numerous depots; at one time they were commonplace on the Great Eastern section. No. 64425 was withdrawn in November 1960.   24.6.56

Opposite, top: J11 no. 64292, seen here at Annesley, was one of the first batch built in 1901 by Neilson, Reid & Company. During its service life it was superheated and reclassified, and was withdrawn in July 1962.   4.4.54

Opposite, bottom: The J11 class 0–6–0s were the Great Central Railway's 'maids of all work'. This is no. 64331, photographed on a dismal grey day at Woodford Halse.   27.3.55

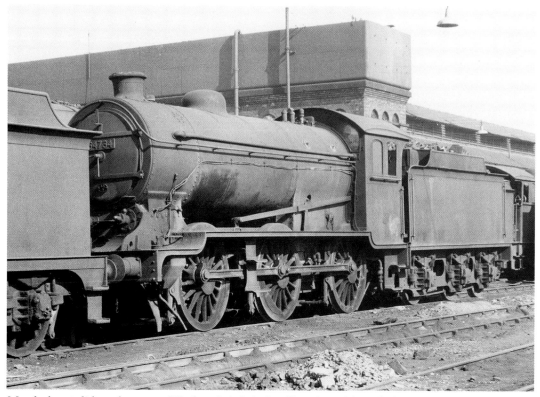

March depot did not have any J39 class 0–6–0s in its allocation, although they were frequent visitors. No. 64734, seen standing near the large water tower, was a Lincoln engine and would have almost certainly worked in via the GN–GE joint line.   13.3.55

J39 no. 64771 was a Stratford engine. Photographed at its home shed, it was in poor external condition. Like many locomotives in their final years, it had such a coating of soot and grime that the cabside number was barely visible.   7.5.55

J39 no. 64722, fresh out of Stratford works after a general overhaul, waits at the running shed prior to returning home to Lincoln depot. The J39 class was a Gresley design introduced in 1926.   7.5.55

J39 no. 64802 was the only member of the class allocated to Melton Constable. I photographed it at Yarmouth Beach, a small shed with just eleven engines allocated to it in 1954.   18.8.59

01 no. 63863 at Annesley. This engine was among the last survivors of the class, spending its final period working from Staveley depot. Built in 1919 for the ROD by the North British Locomotive Company, it was rebuilt to 01 class in September 1945, and served for another twenty years until withdrawn in June 1965.   4.4.54

On Sundays the yards at Annesley depot were full of heavy goods locomotives. 01 no. 63777 is seen here in company with two of its classmates. It remained in service, still allocated to Annesley, until October 1962.   4.4.54

These two views of 01 no. 63784 at Annesley clearly illustrate the work-stained condition of most heavy goods engines. It had presumably received works attention recently as the smokebox and chimney have been repainted. The cabside number had been rubbed over with an oily rag. A sizeable former Great Central Railway depot, Annesley was principally concerned with heavy freight engines and had more than fifty 2–8–0s of classes 01 and 04 allocated to it in the early 1950s. Many of their duties were to Woodford. No. 63784 was an example of the 01 class, which were rebuilds of 04s. This particular engine was built for the government during the First World War and was later purchased by the LNER. 4.4.54

O2/3 class no. 63951 pictured in good external condition at its home shed, Doncaster. The O2/3s were a development of earlier engines, having reduced boiler mountings and a side-window cab. They were to be found at various sheds in the Doncaster district and at Grantham. No. 63951 was withdrawn in June 1962 and ended its days at Doncaster works. 23.9.56

Opposite, top: This O1 engine, no. 63652, was in very poor external condition and its number was not visible. It was photographed at a smoky Woodford Halse depot. Introduced by E. Thompson in 1944, the O1s were rebuilds of O4 class locomotives with 100A-type boilers, Walschaerts valve gear and new cylinders. 27.3.55

Opposite, bottom: A fitter, oil can in his hand, attends to another grimy O1 2–8–0, this time no. 63863, at Woodford Halse shed. O1s were commonplace on the Great Central line. No. 63863 was an Annesley engine; in fact Annesley was home to most of the O1s rebuilt from O4s. 27.3.55

Officially classified 02/3, no. 63955 was a further development of the class. A Doncaster engine, it is seen here at its home depot. It was withdrawn in May 1962 and cut up at Doncaster works the same month.   24.6.56

The 02 class 2–8–0s were originally designed by Gresley but over the years various alterations were made to them. No. 63942, seen here at Doncaster, still had the original cab which offered only limited protection from the elements. Withdrawals commenced in 1960, with the class becoming extinct in 1963. Compare the grimy appearance of the 02 with the gleaming ex-works J50 in the background.   24.6.56

O4 no. 63858 waiting for its next duty at Lincoln, a former Great Northern Railway depot. O4 class locomotives were frequent visitors to this depot but none was allocated there.   26.8.51

No. 63615, pictured at Mexborough, is an O4/7 – a rebuild with an O2-type boiler but retaining its Great Central-type smokebox. This engine was completed at Gorton works in February 1914 as a O4/1 and was rebuilt to O4/7 in December 1939. It remained in service until September 1964, when it was withdrawn from Langwith Junction after eight months in store.   24.6.56

O4/3 no. 63735 was built by the North British Locomotive Company for service in the First World War. Like so many of the O4s, it had steam brake only and no water scoop. These engines were to give many years of excellent service. No. 63735, photographed at Mexborough, was taken into stock in October 1927 and withdrawn in December 1962.   24.6.56

The O4s were extensively used to handle coal traffic from the Nottinghamshire and Yorkshire coalfields. No. 63730 was one of a considerable number allocated to Mexborough shed. Built for the ROD by Robert Stephenson & Company in November 1919, it was rebuilt as an O4/8 after this picture was taken, entering traffic in March 1958 and remaining in service until January 1966.   24.6.56

These four locomotives at Doncaster shed originally worked for the three companies that merged to form the LNER. The cab of no. 61472, an ex-North Eastern B16 4–6–0, can be seen on the far left. Next to it is J52 no. 68835, a Great Northern design. O4/3 no. 63885, an Ardsley engine, was a Robinson/Great Central design built for the ROD and later taken into LNER stock. On the far right is J50 no. 68907, just ex-works, another Great Northern design.   24.6.56

O4/3 no. 63779, photographed from the tender end. The lion and wheel emblem can be clearly seen. No. 63779 was never rebuilt and remained a steam brake only engine until it was withdrawn from Retford in April 1962.   24.6.56

Locomotive no. 63818, photographed at Frodingham, was originally built for the Railway Operating Division during the First World War. It was completed by the North British Locomotive Company at their Queens Park works in July 1918, just a short time before the war ended. It was built as an 04 class with steam brake only and no water scoop. Rebuilt as an 04/8, as seen here in June 1947, it remained in service until April 1966.   25.8.57

Opposite, top: The stark, distinctive features of Frodingham shed can be seen behind 04 class no. 63761. Originally a Great Central depot, Frodingham was one of the last Eastern Region sheds to have an allocation of steam locomotives, closing in February 1966. The North British Locomotive Company built this engine at Hyde Park works in August 1912. In June 1940 it was rebuilt as an 04/7 with a shortened 02-type boiler but still retained its Great Central-type smokebox. Withdrawal came in June 1959.   25.8.57

Opposite, bottom: The classic lines of the Robinson 04 class are clearly illustrated by no. 63572, photographed in grimy external condition at Frodingham. This was the pioneer member of the class, built at Gorton works in September 1911. It was rebuilt to 04/1 in June 1924 and remained as such until withdrawn in November 1959.   25.8.57

Immingham depot was a former Great Central Railway shed. In the early 1950s its allocation consisted of twelve locomotives, including passenger, freight and shunting types. As might be expected, the 04 class was well represented. Two 04/8 class engines are visible in this picture, with no. 63750 nearest the camera. The North British Locomotive Company built this engine in November 1917 for the Railway Operating Division (as no. 1831). It was rebuilt as an 04/8 in October 1952 and withdrawn in March 1964.   25.8.57

Opposite, top: Any list of classic steam locomotives would surely have to include the Great Central Railway's 04 class, which was first introduced in 1911 to the design of J.G. Robinson. Powerful and reliable, they were selected by the government to be used for military purposes in the First World War. They were built at Gorton works and by several private companies. No. 63900, seen here at Immingham, was built at the North British Locomotive Company's Atlas works in November 1919 for the Railway Operating Division, passing into LNER ownership in 1927. It remained an 04/3 throughout its life and remained in service until September 1962.   25.8.57

Opposite, bottom: R. Stephenson & Company was one of the private companies that built the Great Central Railway's 2–8–0 design for the Railway Operating Division in the First World War. No. 63714, pictured at Annesley, was completed by the company in January 1919, just after the war had ended. It entered LNER stock in April 1924 and throughout its service life had steam brake only and no water scoop. It was withdrawn in March 1959.   4.4.54

This locomotive, 2–8–0 no. 63858, started life as an 04/3. Built by the North British Locomotive Company for the ROD in 1919, it was completed nine months after the war had ended. It was taken into LNER stock in June 1927 and in May 1953 it was rebuilt as an 04/8. It is seen here at Doncaster.   7.11.54

04 no. 63618 in a poor external condition at March depot, with the cabside number barely visible. It is a typical example of the 04/1 class. Completed at Gorton works in March 1914, it was fitted with vacuum and steam brake as well as a water scoop. This engine was withdrawn from service in February 1963.   13.3.55

The 04s were repainted in plain black livery following a general overhaul. No. 63634, pictured at New England shed, had recently gone through works and was in good external condition. Note the coal piled high on the tender. Built at Gorton in 1912, this engine was converted to an 04/7 in 1940, with a shortened 02-type boiler but still retaining its Great Central-type smokebox.   13.3.55

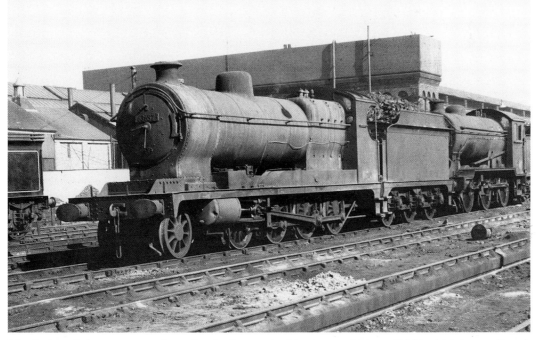

March depot's huge water tank can be clearly seen in this picture of 04 no. 63657, which is standing at an area known to enginemen as the 'old hundred'. This engine was built by Kitson & Company for the Railway Operating Division and was completed in June 1918, later being taken into LNER stock. When this photograph was taken the locomotive was in a work-stained external condition; note the large dent on the cylinder end.   13.3.55

New England WDs and other engines used on heavy freight trains were serviced at Hornsey shed before their return journey. No. 90169 had recently received a general overhaul. Within a short time it would, like its classmates, have a liberal coating of oil and grime.   3.1.54

Opposite, top: WD no. 90506 from March shed blasts through St Ives on a misty autumn morning. The line between March and Cambridge known as the 'St Ives loop' was extensively used by goods trains working to and from London, thus reducing pressure on the direct route.   8.11.52

Opposite, bottom: Heavy coal trains on their way to Ferme Park were a regular sight several times a day during the 1950s. In the early years they were worked by WD 2–8–0s. When the Standard class 9F 2–10–0s arrived at New England they took over some of these duties but they never wholly replaced these very useful engines. No. 90158 is seen here passing Huntingdon.   26.1.53

One of New England depot's WD 2–8–0s, no. 90305, nears Peterborough North station heading a mixed goods for London. At this time WDs were the principal heavy goods locomotives working south of Peterborough but this would change with the arrival of the Standard 9F 2–10–0s.   25.5.51

Opposite, top: WD no. 90722 was a visitor to March; it was a London Midland Region engine from Normanton depot. The ex-WD engines enjoyed a very long association with March, and in the early 1950s fifty members of the class were allocated to the depot. The shed had officially closed to steam by the early 1960s, so any steam locomotives present were visitors.   30.8.64

Opposite, bottom: The WD 2–8–0s were a feature of the East Coast main line throughout the 1950s, and they were to be found at numerous depots until they closed to steam. No. 90675 is pictured at New England the month before it closed.   6.12.64

Overleaf: New England Standard 9F no. 92042 in full cry on its journey north, having been given the main line at Huntingdon. Only at quiet periods would goods trains have a clear run on the Down main as it involved a long 1-in-200 climb.   28.2.63

The New England 9F 2–10–0s replaced many of the depot's WD 2–8–0s, with their principal duties including heavy coal trains to London. Here no. 92149 stands in the yard of a very run-down New England awaiting its next duty.   30.8.64

Standard 9F no. 92180 heads an engineer's train near Huntingdon no. 2 signal-box, ready for weekend work by engineers. These trains usually had a brake van at each end ready for the return working.   24.8.61

3. Tank Locomotives

The majority of the tank engines on the Eastern Region had the 0–6–0 wheel arrangement and they were principally engaged on shunting work, as well as stock working. In the early 1950s suburban traffic in and out of Liverpool Street and Kings Cross was in the hands of class N7 0–6–2Ts, with N2 class engines at Kings Cross. The Thompson L1 class 2–6–4Ts were also to be seen on this work. The ex-Great Eastern 0–6–0Ts that were at one time used on the suburban services were still very much in evidence throughout the 1950s, although principally on stock workings and shunting duties.

In the early 1950s the large tank engines that were designed for hump shunting had mostly been replaced by diesel locomotives. Several of the huge 0–8–4Ts of class S1 were still to be found standing at Doncaster. These monsters, which weighed in at just over 99 tons, were a Great Central design introduced in 1907, with a further two added in 1932. Several examples had been fitted with a booster, but this was later removed. With the sole exception of the class U1 2–8–8–2T Beyer-Garratt, the S1s were the largest tank locomotives to be found on the Eastern Region.

Massive inroads were made into the various classes of ex-Great Eastern 2–4–2Ts in the early 1950s but examples of locomotives introduced by other pre-Grouping railways were still to be found on the Eastern Region at this time. They included the three ex-North Eastern Railway G5 0–4–4Ts working on the Bartlow branch and the ex-Midland 0–6–0T allocated to Doncaster, while Stratford shed had several ex-LTSR 4–4–2Ts standing in the yard.

A class I will always remember is the Ivatt C12 4–4–2Ts. Originally built for suburban workings in the London area, by the 1950s they were mostly confined to branch lines. At Peterborough North they were assigned banking duties, where they blasted through the station assisting the restarting of northbound expresses. One could hardly fail to notice them under the overall roof that existed at that time. Sadly no examples of this 1898 design have survived.

To the north of Huntingdon station there were two derailments in consecutive months. The first involved L1 no. 67740, which became derailed on a crossover, completely closing the main line. Here the New England breakdown crane is preparing to lift the locomotive.   19.5.51

Boston shed had an allocation of two A5 class 4–6–2Ts. One of them was no. 69808, which remained there for most of the 1950s. Withdrawal was in November 1960. It was cut up at Darlington where numerous A5s had received work attention. No. 69808 was among the first batch of these locomotives to be built for working suburban services out of Marylebone.　　　　　13.3.55

The graceful A5 class 4–6–2Ts were used on the Grantham to Nottingham line and other local services. Here, no. 69822 stands ready for work outside Grantham shed. Robinson introduced the A5s for the Great Central Railway in 1911.　　　　　7.8.54

Hitchin L1 2–6–4Ts were regular locomotives on Kings Cross to Peterborough stopping passenger services. In addition, in the mid-1950s they worked a pick-up goods to and from Huntingdon. No. 67741 stands in the yards awaiting its early evening departure. In the mid-1950s wagons from East Anglia were included in the St Ives to Huntingdon goods for onward forwarding.   10.8.54

The L1 class 2–6–4Ts allocated to Hitchin were mainly used on passenger trains to London, Peterborough and Cambridge. As with several other post-war classes, batches were built by private companies. No. 67746, seen here under repair at Hitchin, was built by the North British Locomotive Company in 1948.   14.10.56

Thick smoke hangs in the air at Kings Cross shed as N2 no. 69490 prepares for its next duty. This was the first member of the class to be built at Doncaster, being completed in December 1920. Several others built by the North British Locomotive Company were completed in the same month. The majority of the N2s were built by private companies, three others being involved over the years. No. 69490 was withdrawn in July 1959. 3.1.54

Opposite, top: Despite its neat outward appearance N1 class 0–6–2T no. 69435 had just over a year left in service when I photographed it at Hornsey. This shed had a long association with the class, but all was about to change as the last engine left in 1956. Examples survived in the West Riding for three more years. 3.1.54

Opposite, bottom: Hornsey shed was a sizeable depot with around seventy locomotives, all except ten of which were tank engines used on shunting and stock workings. All the exceptions were J6 class 0–6–0s. All the N1 class 0–6–2Ts working in the London area were Hornsey engines. No. 69467 is seen here ready for its next duty. 3.1.54

N2 class 0–6–2T no. 69515 was fitted with condensing gear when it was built by the North British Locomotive Company in 1921. This equipment was removed in 1928 and never refitted. The engine is seen here at Hitchin shed with J15 no. 65479 behind. The N2 was a Kings Cross engine, and it remained there until it was withdrawn in July 1959.　　　　　　　　　　　　　　　14.10.56

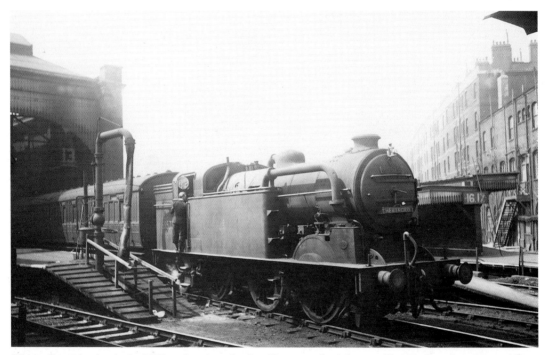

Kings Cross in the early 1950s echoed to the familiar sound of the sturdy N2 class 0–6–2Ts working suburban services and stock workings. No. 69575 is seen here at the head of a Hertford train, with the destination board clearly visible at the base of the locomotive's smokebox. Most of the N2s working in the area were fitted with condensing gear, as shown here.　　　　　　　　　　　　　13.5.51

The sturdy J52 class saddletanks were allocated to many depots. Most of their work involved shunting and pilot duties and they were a common sight. No. 68814, seen here, was a Colwick engine; built at Doncaster in 1897, it remained in service until November 1955.   4.4.54

The once-numerous J52 class was introduced by H.A. Ivatt in 1897, and these engines were a familiar sight in London. No. 68827 is pictured here on a dismal January day at its home shed, Kings Cross. Alongside are examples of the N2 class 0–6–2Ts which were widely used on suburban trains.   3.1.54

Two withdrawn J52s stand forlornly at Doncaster shed, waiting to make their final journey to the works where they would join the scrap road. No. 68791 was built by Neilson & Company in 1896. Behind it is no. 68760, which was built three years earlier; both were fitted with condensing gear. No. 68791 had already lost one of its front buffers.   7.11.54

Opposite, top: Some of the oldest J52s were to be found at Doncaster shed, and no. 68760 was one of them. Completed at Doncaster works in March 1893 and withdrawn in November 1954, this engine was a rebuild of a Stirling locomotive fitted with condensing gear.   9.11.54

Opposite, bottom: The ubiquitous J52 class engines were to be found at numerous depots during the 1950s. No. 68817, photographed at New England, was one of the batch built by R. Stephenson & Company in 1899 for the Great Northern Railway. These were sturdy and powerful engines for their size and were mostly used as yard shunters.   13.3.55

On a rail journey to and from London in the 1950s you would invariably see J50 class engines busily shunting in several yards along the way. At one time twenty-seven were allocated to Hornsey shed, where this picture of no. 68983 was taken.   3.1.54

Peterborough North station had a curve, which meant that northbound express trains that had stopped there required a banker engine to get them under way again. For many years this work was handled by elderly C12 class 4–4–2Ts of Great Northern origin, and no. 67368 is pictured on this duty. I can well remember the sharp exhaust note of these engines echoing back off the overall roof that was present at that time.   5.2.53

C12 no. 67395, seen here at March shed, was allocated to Hull Botanic Garden, a shed that fell under North Eastern Region jurisdiction. The word 'Hull' has been chalked on the side near the footplate. No. 67395 was fitted with one of the taller chimneys.   13.3.55

The C12 class engines were widely used on London suburban services in their heyday but by the 1950s those that remained had been relegated to more mundane duties. No. 67352, seen here, was one of the class pioneers: built in 1898, it had completed sixty years' service when it was withdrawn. 13.3.55

New England was home to several veteran C12 class 4–4–2Ts. They worked variously on local branch line duties, as bankers at Peterborough North and as carriage pilots. This one, no. 67366, was surplus to requirements and had been placed in store. It was subsequently returned to service before being withdrawn in 1958. 13.3.55

The N5 class 0–6–2Ts were to be found in many parts of the Eastern Region. They were a mixed traffic class, originally introduced in 1891. Withdrawals were rapid in the late 1950s and the last engine was withdrawn in 1961. In 1959 eight were allocated to New England, principally for use as station pilots. 24.6.56

Opposite, top: Three C13 class 4–4–2Ts, including no. 67420, were allocated to Neasden, where their principal duties were the Chesham branch auto-trains. All three were withdrawn in December 1958, having been replaced by 2MT 2–6–2Ts shortly after the London Midland Region had taken over. 20.5.55

Opposite, bottom: The Great Central Railway's C13 class 4–4–2s were easily recognisable by their distinctive 'flower-pot' chimneys. Designed by Robinson, the C13s were introduced in 1903. Several engines were fitted for push-pull working. No. 67434 is seen here awaiting its next duty at Mexborough shed. 24.6.56

Its working days over, N4 no. 69231 awaits its fate at Doncaster scrap road. T. Parker introduced the N4 class for the Manchester, Sheffield & Lincolnshire Railway, which later became part of the Great Central. Light was fading rapidly when this picture was taken, but it was the only opportunity I had to photograph an N4.   7.11.54

Opposite, top: Three years after nationalisation locomotives could still be found lettered LNER, as with J68 class no. 8645 seen here on station pilot duties at Cambridge.   30.5.51

Opposite, bottom: Designed principally for suburban use, F6 class locomotives were usually to be found on branch line workings in East Anglia. No. 67236 was a Bury St Edmunds engine. During a visit to Cambridge it was pressed into use as a station pilot.   30.5.51

During the early 1950s Hitchin shed had several interesting locomotives of Great Eastern Railway origin in its allocation. These included J68 no. 68638, together with an E4 2–4–0 and a J15 0–6–0. The latter pair were principally used on the Henlow branch. Note the Westinghouse pump that had evidently received numerous hammer blows over the years.   14.10.56

These two Great Eastern veterans awaiting their fate at Stratford works are F4 no. 67174, fitted with a short stovepipe chimney, and a J70 class tram engine. No. 67174 was built at Stratford in November 1908 and withdrawn in December 1954. As with other Great Eastern designs, the F4s could also be found working in Scotland in BR days.   7.5.55

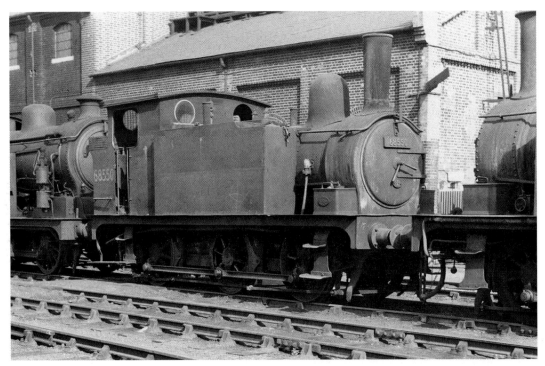

The ex-Great Eastern 0–6–0Ts of class J69 were widely distributed in former LNER territory, with a number serving north of the border. Some were used on passenger duties while others were shunting engines. No. 68550, seen here at Stratford complete with a stovepipe chimney, was one of the latter. Built in 1894, it completed a very commendable sixty-seven years' service before withdrawal.   7.5.55

N7 class engines were extensively used on suburban services out of Liverpool Street and elsewhere. Stratford had a large number in its allocation, including no. 69732, pictured here at its home shed. Sister engine no. 69703 can be seen in the background, together with other members of the class. 7.5.55

The Y4 class was introduced for shunting work where tight curves existed. These sturdy engines were powerful for their size. In total, five were constructed, all of which were built at Stratford works between 1913 and 1921. No. 68125 was the first member of the class, entering service in November 1913. It was also the first to be withdrawn, in September 1955. I photographed it at Stratford; note the dumb buffers to prevent locking on curves, and the coal piled up on the firebox. 7.5.55

Boston depot had a number of tank locomotives for shunting on the docks and elsewhere. These included eight of Great Eastern origin, J67/1 no. 68570 among them. In the shed entrance is J6 no. 64244.   13.3.55

Work was already scarce for these two F6 class 2–4–2Ts seen here in store at Cambridge. Pieces of tarpaulin had been tied over the chimneys to provide protection from the elements. Nearest the camera is no. 67238, with no. 67227 behind.   19.3.55

I remember J66 class no. 68383 shunting at Cambridge over many years. It then moved to Yarmouth (South Town) before the call came for its final visit to Stratford works to await the scrapman's torch. No. 68383 was the last survivor of its class, having been introduced in 1886.   27.3.55

The arrival of diesel shunters resulted in less work for many steam locomotives, including the Q1 class 0–8–0s introduced by Robinson in 1902. This is no. 69934, photographed at Mexborough. Five members of the ten-strong class were withdrawn in 1958, with the remaining five following in 1959. All were cut up at Darlington.   24.6.56

The Q1 class 0–8–0Ts were all rebuilds of ex-Great Central Q4 0–8–0s built between 1902 and 1910. Rebuilding was carried out under Edward Thompson in 1942–5 for heavy shunting duties. They were distributed widely, and during the early 1950s two were to be found at Eastfield shed, Glasgow. No. 69934 is seen here at Frodingham shed, which had seven Q1s in its allocation. No. 69934 remained in service until August 1959.   25.8.57

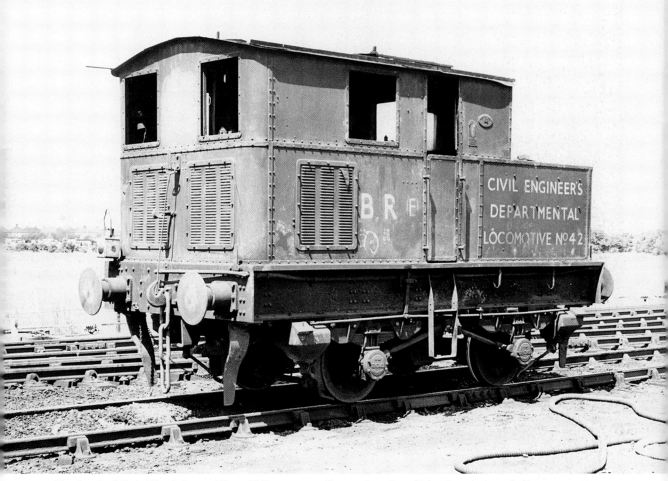

The Sentinel 0–4–0Ts of classes Y1 and Y3 were usually employed on light shunting work. Some were allocated to departmental stock, as was the case with D42, which shunted at the Chesterton permanent way depot near Cambridge. The Sentinel Wagon Works built D42 in 1930, and it was withdrawn from departmental stock in July 1960.   23.6.57

Opposite, top: In 1907 a large new hump marshalling yard was opened by the Great Central Railway at Wath-on-Dearne. Powerful locomotives were required to handle the heavy shunting work, and consequently J.G. Robinson introduced the massive S1 class 0–8–4Ts. Four were built in 1907/8 and were followed by two more in 1932. By 1953 work for them was scarce and several S1s were placed in store at Doncaster, including no. 69902. Withdrawal came in January 1956.   7.11.54

Opposite, bottom: After a lengthy period in store at Doncaster no. 69901 was sent to Frodingham. It remained there until withdrawn, together with no. 69905. With their destruction the class became extinct. Two S1s spent a number of years shunting at March Whitemoor yards, but their duties were taken over by diesel shunters in 1949. No. 69904, also seen in this picture, was withdrawn in January 1956.   7.11.54

Sentinel also built class Y3 Departmental no. 5 in September 1930. It was in normal running stock for ten years until February 1948, and was engaged in departmental service. This picture was taken at Doncaster, where this locomotive was normally employed at the wagon works.   7.11.54

Opposite, top: On one of my visits to March shed I was delighted to find these tram locomotives, formerly used on the Wisbech & Upwell Tramway. There were three J70 0–6–0Ts, no. 68217 and two others, as well as a solitary example of the 0–4–0T Y9 class. The cowcatcher can be clearly seen in this picture, and the valve gear and coupling rods are also visible as the side cover had been taken off.   8.11.52

Opposite, bottom: Several of these 3P 4–4–2Ts were allocated to Tilbury shed, which was transferred from London Midland control to the Eastern Region in 1949. No. 41952 was officially a Tilbury engine, although, along with several others, it was stored at Stratford where this picture was taken.   7.5.55

During the 1950s you could often find locomotives at work far from their usual haunts. This was the case with three ex-North Eastern Railway G5 4–4–0Ts which were allocated to Cambridge depot and worked the Bartlow branch. This was the end of the road for no. 67269, seen here at Doncaster, as it was on its way to Darlington works for scrap.   23.9.56

A stranger in the camp, this veteran ex-Midland Railway 0–6–0T no. 41779 was an Eastern Region engine allocated to Doncaster. The engine still retained its round-topped boiler and Salter safety valves, although it had received an all-over cab.   24.6.56